"Michele Serros is part of a generation of younger w... are fast breaking past old-school notions of identity and style. Wit and irony are her faithful companions, a tender compassion her literary and spiritual compass. She lets us know that cultural confusion—which is as American as it is Chicano—is something to celebrate and embrace. Her writing is fun, funny, hip, and suddenly sad, but never pretentious—the perfect writer to accompany through tense and troubled times."

—Rubén Martínez, author of *The Other Side: Notes from the New L.A., Mexico City, and Beyond*

"Serros treats her subject matter without a trace of condescension and has enormous affection for her characters. She has a knack for going right to the humor and truth of every situation. The world she creates in *Chicana Falsa* is one that's unique in American letters." —Carolyn See, author of *Dreaming: Hard Luck and Good Times in America*

"The voice of Michele Serros sings and mourns and dances inside a cultural spectrum of beauty and pain. These poems and stories bloom from a universe that nurtures and represses, that embraces and attacks, that denies and celebrates the paradoxes of her being. Michele Serros meets the interpersonal and cultural challenges of our time with a tender and critical eye, a soothing voice, a fluid emotional insight. . . . Lyrical, sensuous, and deeply sensitive, *Chicana Falsa* is an excellent and necessary expansion of the literary canon of American women."

—Michèlle T. Clinton, author of *Good Sense & The Faithless*

"Contemporary literary comadre. Michele Serros is a fresh and energetic writer of unparalleled family stories."

—Denise Chávez, author of *Face of an Angel*

"The gift that Michele Serros has is the ability to write about the cruel turns in life that all of us face, regardless of race or class, and to deliver the message in a way that we can still laugh at the irony of it. The crystal clarity of her images makes her universal."

—Montserrat Fontes, author of *First Confession* and *Dreams of the Centaur*, winner of the American Book Award

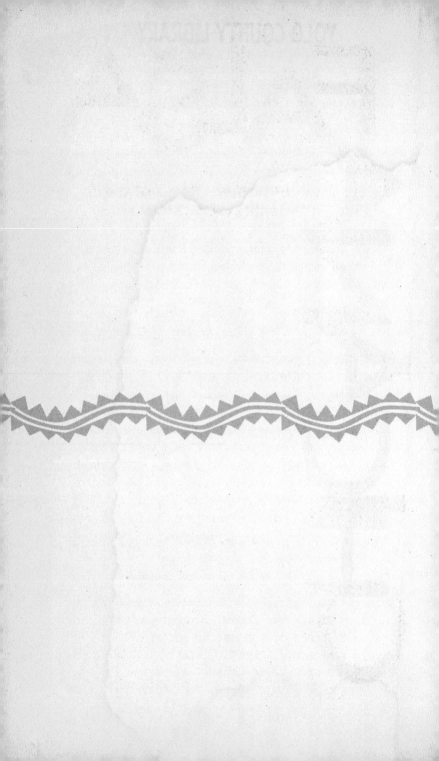

CHICANA FALSA

and other stories of death,
identity, and Oxnard

MICHELE SERROS

RIVERHEAD BOOKS • NEW YORK

Riverhead Books
Published by The Berkley Publishing Group
A division of Penguin Putnam Inc.
375 Hudson Street
New York, New York 10014

First published by Lalo Press 1993
Lalo Press trade paperback ISBN: 1-886827-00-1
First Riverhead trade paperback edition: June 1998

The Penguin Putnam Inc. World Wide Web site address is
http://www.penguinputnam.com

The Library of Congress Cataloging-in-Publication Data

Serros, Michele M.
    Chicana falsa, and other stories of death, identity, and Oxnard /
  Michele M. Serros.—1st Riverhead trade pbk. ed.
      p.   cm.
    ISBN 1-57322-685-8
    1. Mexican American women—Literary collections.   2. Mexican
Americans—Literary collections.   I. Title.
PS3569.E733C48   1998
810.8'09287'0896872073—dc21
                                                                97-32048
                                                                CIP

Printed in the United States of America

10   9   8   7   6   5

To my Mom

CONTENTS

Acknowledgments   *ix*

Introduction   *xi*

La Letty   *1*

Annie Says   *4*

Dead Pig's Revenge   *7*

Shower Power Hippie Man   *12*

Disco Gymnasium   *15*

What Is Bad   *17*

Tag Banger's Last Can   *21*

Attention Shoppers   *22*

White Owned   *26*

What Boyfriend Told Me at Age Seventeen   *28*

Mi Problema   *31*

JohnwannabeChicano   *33*

The Day My Sister Was on Television   *35*

El Cielo or Bust   *39*

A Belated Victory (for Us)   *42*

Dear Diary   *46*

The Superhero Scam   *48*

Stuff   *50*

Mr. and Mrs. White Guilt   *55*

Mr. BOOM BOOM Man   *57*

The Real Me   *60*

The Best Years of My Life   *61*

Planned Parenthood: Age Sixteen   *64*

The Grudge-Holders   *66*

Manos Morenas   *71*

The Gift   *73*

ACKNOWLEDGMENTS

Much gratitude to poet and writer Michelle T. Clinton. Her support and guidance not only gave me the confidence to put words on paper but the courage to finally share them with others.

Thank you to all the writers in the Women's Multicultural Poetry Workshop at the Beyond Baroque Literary/Arts Center, especially Nancy Agabian, Maria Cabildo, Alison Hatter, Ralph Seaton, and Pam Ward.

Thanks, Betsy, for your advice and kindness!

Much appreciation to everyone's favorite professor and writer, Daniel Cano, as well as to Adela Carrasco for friendship and photocopying favors.

Love to Gene (my dream) Trautmann.

And as always, a special thanks to Leticia "La Letty" Maria for the tag and title of the book.

INTRODUCTION

It was just one of those days. The beginning of May and I was in the quad area of Santa Monica College going over geometry homework when I just *knew*. I had to call home. Something was wrong. Five minutes later I was dialing my mama's phone number and an aunt answered. She confirmed my feeling.

"Yes," she said slowly. "Your mother's back in the hospital. Maybe you should come home . . . for a while."

"A while" turned into a couple of days, then a couple of weeks. My mama was dying. On Mother's Day a doctor gave us the amount of time she had left. My family and I camped out in the hospital waiting room, trying our best to ignore all the Mother's Day commercials that blasted from the waiting room's TV. I can't think of a worse time in my life. My skin broke out, my scalp sprouted dandruff and friends bailed. ("I wanted to call, but I just didn't know what to say.") Four days later, my mama died.

I was appointed to write her obituary. I was the so-called writer of the family, and this was to be my first published piece. When I described my mother as an artist, someone questioned it. "Are you sure you want to say that? I mean, it isn't like she sold anything. Not like she had her art up in galleries or anything. She wasn't an artist, really."

These accusations stung. Here was a definition of an artist. Someone who just didn't make art, but who was recognized for it. Someone who just didn't sell art, but made good money from it. Definitions have always played a big part in my life: a true Mexican versus a fake Mexican, a good student versus a lousy one, a true artist versus a wannabe one. Nonetheless, my mama would have been crushed knowing she left this earth not remembered as an artist. It was her fear and lack of confidence that kept her art stuck on an easel, hidden away in the corner of our family's garage.

When I lost my mama, I believed nothing could be more horrible. I felt nothing in the world could harm or threaten me as much as her leaving. But it was her death that gave me the courage to finally share some of my own poems and stories. What more could I possibly lose? I suddenly felt emotionally empowered.

These stories have clung to the back of my mind for years. They were finally written while still a student at Santa Monica College, then published a year later at a small press when I was an undergrad at UCLA.

The purpose? To make someone happy, inspired. Maybe make someone who hated to read actually enjoy a book. That, and I guess I just couldn't bear the thought of someone questioning what my own obituary would say.

Michele Serros
Spring 1998

CHICANA FALSA

LA LETTY

Her steady hand
outlines inside bottom eyelid,
thick
darkening to deep velvet black.
A finishing touch
ends sixty minute routine
for this raccoon eyed beauty.
Turning from the mirror
she says:
"You know what you are?
                    A Chicana Falsa."

"MEChA don't mean shit,
and that sloppy Spanish of yours
will never get you any discount at Bob's market."

"HOMOGENIZED HISPANIC,
that's what you are."

She
had once been "Leticia,"
"Tish" for short,
but now
only two weeks into junior high,
She is "La Letty"
y que
no mas.

Taught me
years ago,
how to ride a bike.
Doesn't matter now
Chevy Impalas snatch
her from school,
Mexican Cadillacs
low and slow,
done up in candy paint, metal flake
chrome-plated spoke rims
glistening.
Young boys
in hair nets and Dickies
fingers dipped in Old English ink
controlled
chained steering wheels
and La Letty.
Steered her
away from me,
my sister, best friend.
And she fell for them
for it,
the whole creased-khaki
pressed-flannel
medallion-wearing scene.

Every night
after dinner was done
TV clicked off
in Holly Hobbie haven
my naked lids closed
as I listened for
soft car hum

copycat teenage laughter
faint oldies station . . .
waiting
and waiting
for Tish
        to come home.

ANNIE SAYS

My tia Annie told me:
"You could never be a writer,
let alone a poet.
What do you know?
I mean, what can you write about?

"You got a D on your last book report
you gotta be able to write English good,
use big words . . .
and you've never even been out of Oxnard.
Writers travel
all the time
New York, Paris, Rome . . .
Every place they make Oil of Olay.
That's where writers go,
that's where they live.
Your family doesn't have money to travel.
You never will.
And you don't even type.
Now, how you gonna be a writer?
Sure, some famous poets,
they say
wrote longhand
but that was long ago,
and they were men.
Men have it so easy,
worthless lazy dogs.
But you wouldn't know about that
'cause you've never been with one.

You've never
ate,
slept,
inhaled,
pure passionate love.
Writers are always in love,
like this *Harlequin* romance I'm reading.
Now, how are you gonna be a writer?
You don't even like boys yet.
You've never given your heart to a boy,
so he could take it,
hold it,
clench it,
wring it dry,
to toss away,
forgotten in the gutter.

"They make you cry,
hurt,
suffer.
Writers know stuff like that,
they heal their pain with words.
You don't know about pain,
anguish,
outrage,
protest.
Look on TV . . .
The Brown Berets,
they're marching.
The whole Chicano movement
passing you by and
you don't even know about that.
You weren't born in no barrio.
No tortilleria down your street.

Bullets never whizzed
past your baby head.

"Chicana Without a Cause.

"No, mi'ja,
Nobody will ever buy your books,
so put your pencil down
and change the channel for me,
it's time for *As the World Turns*."

DEAD PIG'S REVENGE

I knew every time
Dad packed us up
to travel the distance
from Oxnard to Chino
my family would eat good.
We would eat free
'cuz fave uncle Vincent
was a restaurateur,
a professional businessman,
proud owner of
a catering truck.
A coach as in
Super-rico taco
mariachi blaring
expired license plates
loncheria,
but a nice one.

He always dreamed of
one day owning his own business,
becoming a self-employed man,
his own boss,
soccer on Sundays,
sleeping off hangovers
on Monday.
He loved those short workweeks.
So finally after scraping up
what little money he had,

he got the coach.
It helped Johnny,
his fourth kid, get through college,
kept Aunt Dolly up all night,
chopping
and chopping,
cilantro,
onions,
tomatoes,
with dull knives.
His place had everything
any fine establishment had:
sesos,
lenguas,
tripas
and my favorite,
              chicharrones.

My mother always warned:
"That's solid lard,
pure grease.
That poor dead pig's
gonna have revenge on you yet,
make you fat,
make you fart,
scatter your skin with
white-tipped pimples.
No man's gonna want you."
Her weak threats
didn't work.
Man, couldn't get enough
of that crackly pork skin.
I crammed them in tortillas
that were always too small,

so I ate them right out of the pot,
throwing small crispy bits into the air,
like popcorn,
letting them land
in my open anxious mouth.
I used to eye
my cousin Amy's pet piglet.
With a wink I'd say,
"See you in a couple of years . . .
in my belly!"
That'd send Amy crying into the house.

One ordinary visit
while I sat in the coach's shade
I could see my father
talking chickens with Uncle Vincent,
my mother inside with Aunt Dolly.
I was shoving my dear chicharrones
into my mouth.
Something happened.
They stayed right there,
in my throat.
I swallowed hard to help them down,
coughed firmly to help them up,
but they wouldn't budge.
I could feel coarse pig hairs
tickle my throat,
but I wasn't laughing.
This was not funny.
I couldn't breathe.
I was going to DIE!
My mother was right,
the dead pig's revenge!
I was going to DIE.

My father
was suddenly miles away . . .
Thoughts raced through my mind,
who'll take care of Miss Rosie,
my pet goat?
Still haven't got "Student of the Month."
But more agonizing than
any of these things,
than any of this,
I thought of the headline,
the headline in my obituary:

Chicharrones Choke Chicana Child to Death (in Chino)

Oh my god,
I couldn't die with a headline like that!
The humiliation.
I didn't want to die.
I wanted to live!
I wanted to live!
My legs lost balance . . .
I was getting no more air
Suddenly a thud.
It was dark.

I woke up to find
Cousin Amy above me.
"You were turning blue,
so I punched you on the back
like they do on TV."
That night Amy got her favorite dinner.
My mom and dad
shook their heads in disgust,
hearing her repeat the story

over and over again.
But I didn't care,
I was alive!
I was free!
to walk,
to breath,
to think,
to eat.
I stepped out to the backyard
walked over to the caged pen
to watch over Amy's sleeping piglet.
It was so full of life
a beautiful breathing thing
I spent all night with it.
Watching,
thinking,
waiting,
    salivating.

SHOWER POWER HIPPIE MAN

He bathed twice a day. Lydia, Patty, Goony and I caught his second act every other evening at 6:45 PM. We called him "shower power" 'cause unlike our own fathers and brothers, he showered twice in one day . . . long hot twenty minute showers. I'd never heard such a thing, guess no one ever pounds on his bathroom door. We tagged him "hippie" 'cause his hair was long, almost reaching his shoulders. No men in our neighborhood had such hair. We had so called "real men," as Cousin Amy used to say, with hair that was short, black and slicked all the way back . . . that's what real men were made of.

Nonetheless, three times a week, with bellies full of Hamburger Helper, tacos and KFC dinner packs, the four of us would gather in front of my home, to walk the six blocks into the "other neighborhood" to visit our man. We'd walk up our street, Cortez Avenue, down Cerritos Place, left on Citrus Drive till we reached it, his street, Manzanita Lane.

Slipping behind his garage, into his alley, we ignored barking dogs, the cries of horny tomcats, back porch lights, and helped each other over dented garbage cans to climb onto his high concrete wall. We'd wait, watching that curtainless bathroom window till finally he'd enter.

Then, there he was, our man, tall, pink, and freckled, a dingy white motel towel cradling low on his pale man hips. Sometimes he'd have a transistor radio, and with closed eyes and clenched fist he'd start to sing that song he wrote just for us, "There's a lady whose sure all that glitters is gold . . ." We loved when our Shower Power Hippie Man sang for us. But the best was yet to come. Goony would make her usual tongue drum roll in anticipation and, seconds later, the hip hugging towel was off! I mean right off, at his ankles and there he was, for all four of us to see. Our nine-year-old eyes followed hairy hippie butt into cracked mildew shower stall. Lather from watered down No More Tears trickled down to body parts we were much too young to pronounce. He loved to wash "down there," you know, *it* and he'd yank up his droopy *it* thing to soap up pink, furry private flesh.

Yes, he did make bathing a joy. He was truly our man, no wait, he was our *boyfriend*. We were too good for all the 5th grade boys at Rio Real Elementary. We were the cool girls with the big secret, and we promised to keep it that way till the day we died. It was our pact, and we followed it, *big time*.

One Sunday evening as we waited, at our usual time, he walked into his bathroom. He seemed different right away. No transistor, no hop to his walk. He quickly got into the shower, first lathering his arms, chest, and *it*. He spent a lot of time lathering *IT*. "What do you think he's doing?" asked Lydia. None of us answered.

He kept yanking and pulling, pulling and yanking, and slowly, like Tia Annie's Boston terrier, it stood up, stood out, stood red, different from any other body part we'd ever seen in our lives. An alien tentacle from another planet. He continued to lather. "Don't you think it's clean by now?" Goony asked. Nobody answered. Shower Power Hippie Man's face slowly grew violent, and anger began to envelope his usual calm. And suddenly, like the volcano in the film we saw in Mr. Larkey's geography class, he exploded. I mean, right then and there in his shower, in his house, in front of us, in front of our horrified eyes. Thick Twinkie cream ringlets spurted here, there, everywhere. Patty covered her mouth, but it was way too late, her scream reached his window and Hippie Man spun his head sideways to look out toward *US*. Naked and dripping with water, he made his way toward the open window and *WE* made our way down the trash cans, FAST! Tore down the alley, past barking dogs, kitty cat sex sounds, onto Manzanita, down to Citrus, back on Cerritos Place, and finally, finally, back to Cortez Avenue, where, slowed to an exhausted walk, our cushioned Wallabee soles treaded on familiar home pavement. Our neighborhood trees and graffitied street signs welcomed us back.

We were home, nobody said anything, nobody asked anything. After an over-the-shoulders-quick-and-casual, "See ya tomorrow," we went into our separate homes, to creep by passed out fathers on La-Z-Boy recliners, mother's filling *Bionic Woman* lunch pails, down picture framed hallways, into our grammar school girl bedrooms, to climb into bed, fully clothed, to think about what we had just seen, and to think about those 5th grade boys we would definitely talk to the next day at school.

DISCO GYMNASIUM

The eighteen inch waist
    buxom blonde
informs me,
    "You're late!
        Bathrooms are a mess!"
I tell her,
    "No, I'm no cleaning lady
    I go here, I'm a member."
Her left eyebrow arches
    with suspicion
she checks my plastic card
    proof and signature,
            annoyed wave,
            allows me in.

Feeling very intrusive
in this exclusive
gym,
no bobby socks
or baggy shorts
like Rio De Valle Jr. High
P.E. Class,
I'm the solo *mexicana*
in loose *chongo*
ex-boyfriend's sweatpants
oversize T-shirt
fashion outcast
creating a nuisance

to iridescent,
        pearlescent,
                adolescents!
spandex,
        latex,
                triple X!
Ahead and behind
my eyes can't hide from
the neon green thong thang
dividing large curd
twin cheeks.

It's the Friday afternoon
last ditch effort
to get it on
and get it off
with wealthy white westside women
sweating to inner city rap boys
                (like they secretly do at home).

Kick,
        higher!
Stretch
        longer!
Squeeze
        tighter
DIE
        sooner!

and the whole time
I am thinking of
that double cheese
chimichanga supreme
I'm gonna pick up
on the way home.

WHAT IS BAD

Donna Rodriguez is bad.
More than bad
she has the power
the kind of power
that gets respect
the kind of respect
I envy.

Every Monday morning
like a movie star
encased by tinted windows
her black Trans-Am
pulls up into employee lot
takes up two spaces,
nobody dare complain.

Now that is *BAD*.

All the employees,
men, women alike
part the way
heads humbly bow
so Donna can make her way
to the company time clock.
Suit of armor she wears well
fifty lbs. extra flesh
padding a forty-eight double-D brassiere
sweat rings saturating size 29 blouse.

She slowly strolls by,
petite crucifix sways on a chain
sharing space with a gold plated
self proclamation:
100% BITCH
diamond chip
dotting the "i."

Now that is *BAD*.

At lunch break
the Anglo women shudder in fear
as Donna whips out Weight Watchers Mexi–cuisine.
She's on a diet (again).
It's gonna be a long week.
They pretend to be her friend
get on her good side early
ask about Hector,
her 19 year old baby behind bars,
the red press on nails,
and does she have a good recipe for salsa?

Donna knows their game.
Stays silent
takes long slow drags
off Marlboro Lites
her eyes squint
judging their sloppy eyeliner
creaseless corduroys
tofu tacos.

After letting out a post battle yawn
she heads back to her cubicles
plural,

while all us are crammed
into pet size squares,
Donna gets two
all for herself,
"I'm a big woman.
I need bigger space."
And she gets it,
just like that.

Now that is *BAD*.

The boss is terrified of her.
It's rumored
he recently saw *Zootsuit* on Showtime
and with her white eye shadow
penciled in brows
baby tattoo
nestled between thumb and finger
he suspects she could have
been
might very well still be
a *'chuca*,
as in *pachuca*,
a nonexistent breed
in his Westside life
but here she is
now
living large in the workplace
his workplace,
and he doesn't want any trouble.
Mr. Equal Opportunity Employer,
and scared.

Scared of Donna
who gets weekends off
extended lunches
advance loans
leaves work early on Fridays
to make it to bank,
writes in own hours
on time card.

Now that is *bad*.
That's respect.
And I want it.

TAG BANGER'S LAST CAN

Flaco held his manhood
steady.
Aimed it at
a city block
pissing boosted Krylon
citrus yellow
cherry red
black.

His defiant stand
earned him
a loyal crew
customized baseball cap
TV tabloid exposé
and a toe tag.

Discrimination breeds in the Ralph's supermarket on Venice and Overland. Not in employee opportunities, race, age or sex. Nothing like that, but rather in the temperature controlled depths of the frozen food section. My classmate, Martina, pointed this out to me one day.

She and I were both on aisle nine, going for mixed frozen vegetables. We were making Spanish Rice for a big fundraiser later that night. Now Martina was no cook. She was an activist. Maybe what you'd call militant and maybe what you'd call serious, but still, I liked to hang out with her. She was smart. Anyway, the vegetables make it, you know, colorful, festive like. And since we both thought Veg-All was gross and there was no way we were gonna cut down carrots to micro-mini cubes or pick peas out of their casings like her mama does, frozen veggies would have to do.

Seconds after she opened the glass door Martina said: "Look! Look at this!" She pulled out two frosted bags from the bottom compartment.

"*Malibu Style Vegetables*. And, check this out, *Latino Style Vegetables*, as if we all eat alike . . . I've never seen this . . . Man, even in the lousy freezer they divide and they discriminate!"

"Martina," I asked her, "they're vegetables. How can they be discriminating? Get real."

She went on: "Man, you don't even see it. You're so, so unaware. Look, look at this picture. *Latino Style Vegetables*, they have the vegetables cut up all small. Like, what's that supposed to mean? Like, little food for little people, little minds, little significance? . . . And this *Malibu* kind, the broccoli, the carrots, are cut up large, all big and grand, like 'of great worth,' or something. The cauliflower, which is WHITE, is the biggest vegetable in the picture, over-powering all the rest."

"Oh, Martina," I told her, "you're seeing something that just isn't there. You're crazy to get so worked up over veg-etables. Now just grab a bag and let's go."

"I'm *not* crazy," she protested. "This is how it starts. And look, look at this, the *Latino Style Vegetables* are all spilling out of this wicker basket, all overflowing, messy like. Insin-uating that *we* are overflowing, overcrowding what they think is *their* land. And what's with this wicker basket? You know, we don't use baskets to cart our food around. The *Malibu Style Vegetables* are all neat and in order, properly arranged in a nice WHITE porcelain crock. No problem-causing vegetables here. They're orderly, dignified."

"Dignified vegetables? Martina, is there such a thing?" I was getting so embarrassed. People were starting to look at us.

She was no longer paying attention. I had lost her to her newfound cause. She continued to prove her point.

". . . and look at this, the packaging. *Malibu Style* kind is labeled 'From Ralph's *Private* Selection.' Private, as in 'Not everyone is welcome, no entry to YOU, especially *you*, wet-back. Go back!' "

By this time a small crowd had formed. Everyone was listening to Martina. She didn't care, she continued, "*Malibu Style* are twice as expensive as *Latino Style*. Why? Are they better vegetables? Did white people from Malibu pick them themselves? Did they take off from some corporate meeting early or leave the tennis court midgame to fly up north, put on their designer jeans to get on their hands and knees to pick their own kind of vegetables? Did they? Did they?"

Martina waved the bags over her head and then flung them to the ground. The crowd cheered as an array of green, orange and white exploded on the supermarket floor. She stomped on the soggy newly *integrated* vegetables, mashing them into the linoleum.

And then this extraordinary thing happened. One by one people started to pull frozen produce bags out of the freezer compartments. I saw a Korean woman and her two children stomp on *Oriental Style Vegetables*, a young guy in cowboy boots kicked *Country Style Vegetables* down the aisle toward the checkout lines, and a handsome, dark-haired man ripped apart a bag of *Italian Style Vegetables*. More and more people began to pull bags out of the compartments and destroy the corporate invention of "stereotypes in a bag."

Martina stood back by the Sarah Lee frozen desserts to enjoy the beauty of the revolt she had created. But her clenched-fist victory was soon interrupted. An angry and overweight manager pushed his way though the crowd and ordered a breakup. "You," he said, pushing his finger into Martina's chest, "are trying to incite a riot in MY store. You see this here?" He pointed to his name badge, which stated: Bob G. Smith—Store Director. "*I'm* in charge here. I want you to take your friend and get out of here, NOW!"

Martina picked up our plastic hand basket and threw our other groceries onto the floor. The crowd cheered even louder. She looked straight into the store manager's eye and said, "Man, take your finger out of my face. I'd rather shop at Pavilions than come back to your sorry store! You have a lot to learn, Mr. Store Director!" Martina then grabbed my arm and pulled me through the crowd. Suddenly, I didn't feel like leaving. This was exciting! I pulled back and asked, "Hey, why are we leaving now? I mean, things are just starting to happen! We could snag a bag of frozen fries or some ice cream. Maybe we'll even get arrested!" Martina stopped and turned around. She looked even more furious. She then looked straight into *my* eyes and said, "This isn't about excitement, free food, or getting on TV . . . Man, *you* really have a lot to learn." She let my arm drop, broke through the crowd and headed for the front glass doors. She left behind a new revolution of liberated consumers, the vegetables we no longer needed, no longer wanted and left behind *me*, thinking just how smart she really is.

WHITE OWNED

for Guillermo Gomez-Peña

Pink mama tugs at pink baby.
"Don't wander off,"
she warns.
I sympathize
like any hopeful mother to be.

"You never know,"
pink mama says,
"people today are crazy
just crazy,
        . . .'specially the Spanish."

"You mean people
from Spain?"
I ask.

"No,
Spanish people
              . . . from Mexico.
They snatch white babies
drag 'em across the border
for pornography,
slave labor,
        human sacrifice."

Unemployment lines are long,
rent is months overdue
outspoken counter service

means immediate
            termination.
So I stay silent
wrap her dry-cleaned clothes
in airtight plastic,
watch pink mama and child walk away,
holding the knot in my stomach
and wonder if white boyfriend
will give me beige baby
everyone thinks I stole.

WHAT BOYFRIEND TOLD ME AT AGE SEVENTEEN

"Seven years old
when Uncle Eddie
threw me across the S.D. border,
landing us both in T.J.
My eyes witnessed
dark-skinned
legless men
paddling their way
on pink plastic skateboards
through the thick crowd
of drunk college kids,
gold-toothed vendors,
young girls
pinching puss
out of boyfriend's back,
spray-painted mules
with blood-stained hooves
and three feet high
serape-covered women
rocking their meal tickets to sleep.
Uncle Eddie
threw thirty cents down
for three tacos
and announced,
'This is your culture,
these are your roots
now lay in it.'
Then he laughed . . . at me.

"Seventeen years old,
now high school counselor
Mr. A through M
puts his certificate of
psychology to use,
'College is unthinkable'
he tells me
'you better do The Service,
at the rate you people
are killing each other
you'll be lucky
to get out of high school
ALIVE.'
The blaring red light,
breaks through his office blinds.
Another hair-netted kid
wrong pair of numbers
tattooed on brown belly
being dragged away
to waiting police car.
Mr. A through M
announces,
'This is your culture.
These are your roots.
Now lay in it.'
He then shakes his head
and laughs . . . at me.

"I prefer
ditching 7th period
Econ. class
hiding out
in the football bleachers
getting in touch with my culture

my way
with Lydia the Loadie
Bonnie the Braindead,
smoking cheap Mexican sinse'
taking Physical Graffiti
over territorial graffiti
watching the same
pimply cheerleaders
practice summer camp routines
over
and over again.

"This is my culture,
my entertainment,
nothing to laugh over,
This is me."

MI PROBLEMA

My sincerity isn't good enough.
Eyebrows raise
when I request:
"Hable mas despacio, por favor."
My skin is brown
just like theirs,
but now I'm unworthy of the color
'cause I don't speak Spanish
the way I should.
Then they laugh and talk about
mi problema
in the language I stumble over.

A white person gets encouragement,
praise,
for weak attempts at a second language.
"Maybe he wants to be brown
like us."
and that is good.

My earnest attempts
make me look bad,
dumb.
"Perhaps she wanted to be white
like THEM."
and that is bad.

I keep my flash cards hidden
a practice cassette tape
not labeled
'cause I am ashamed.
I "should know better"
they tell me
"Spanish is in your blood."

I search for S.S.L. classes,
(Spanish as a Second Language)
in college catalogs
and practice
with my grandma.
who gives me patience,
permission to learn.

And then one day,
I'll be a perfected "r" rolling
tilde using Spanish speaker.
A true Mexican at last!

JOHNWANNABECHICANO

John Michael Smith, III is
a Chicano.
Every morning is awakened
by KOXD
the local oldies station,
pockets his blond hair
into black hair net,
stuffs skinny pink legs
into stiff beige khakis,
severely creased.

He is now ready for McKinley Jr. High,
the first school
in prestigious Belmont Estates
to attempt busing,
the second year
of his new identity.

At the breakfast table
he slurps canned *menudo*
ignoring his mother's French toast
and John Michael Smith, II's
stinging silence.

Leaving the house for school
he doesn't look back
as his mother calls out.
Exasperated,

she finally yells:
"Juan!
"Juan Miguel,
you forgot your lunch!"
But he ignores that too.
He's been humiliated
one too many times
in front of his homeboys
by her chicken salad, Ambrosia Surprise
tucked into lime green Tupperware.
Besides,
today the guys
are taking him to "the coach"
for *tacos de sesos*,
whatever that is.

He peddles his lowered Schwinn Stingray
past rows of mini mansions,
lawn jockeys,
leaf blowers attached
to the backs of dark-skinned gardeners.

"¡Hola!
¡Buenas Dias!"
John Michael yells out.
He waves.
They are his people.

His new familia.
He is happy.
He is smug.
He is a Chicano.

THE DAY MY SISTER WAS ON TELEVISION

My Mama let me stay home from school that day. Neighborhood pals, Patty, Goony and Cha-Cha, made their mamas let them ditch also. It wasn't everyday that someone in the neighborhood was going to be on national television. Not just someone. My sister, ultra dream of a teen mentor. We laid out carrot sticks, Fun-Yums, poured Dr. Pepper into glasses with *round* ice cubes. I brought out a tray of my famous cheese baloney rolls, then sprawled my eleven year old body on brown low cut carpet. (Shag carpet gathered hairs and was harder to keep clean.)

Everyone came to our house that day. Neighbor Nosey Nellie for once snapped her blinds SHUT and actually *came out* of her house to watch the action. Fat Fabiola, my mother's second cousin, took over the La-Z-Boy and asked "Is this all the food you're gonna have? Your daughter is gonna be on television and this is what you serve?" Charlie Romero, Patty's dad and the tallest Mexican on the block, dragged himself in with last minute debated jealously. Since he was over six feet tall with a "really good voice," he felt if any Mexican deserved to be on television it should be him. Back in his college days he had the starring role in a student production of *The Pearl*. He was the star of the neighborhood, until now.

Our nineteen inch television set flourished in technicolor and brilliant sound, taking over the whole living room and drowning out our excited chatter. The show my sister was going to star on was beginning. We ignored opening credits, first batch commercials and all other bit players until finally

35

my mother announced: "Ay! Here she comes!" The time *had* come and my sister was going to be introduced on the air. Can you imagine? Her own introduction on national television.

"Eeeeeeee-von Serrrrrrrrrrrrros, come on down! You're our next contestant on *The Price Is Right!*"

Amid back slaps and high fives my sister side stumbled in chunky Cherokee sandals past fellow audience members to make her way down the rust colored aisle. Our TV screen glowed with viewer at home excitement. My sister was now a part of contestant row. Her left breast was covered with a large proud yellow name tag. Her face: flustered red, plucked arched fishwire brows that made her look *chola*, (but she wasn't one really), feathered Farrah hair and lips I knew had three layers of cherry lip balm. She was all I wanted to be someday, especially the part being on television.

The first item to bid on was a deluxe extra heavy duty large load capacity washing machine. Nosey Nellie said "Oh, that's a fancy one. That's like the one Emma on the street behind me got. I happened to be out in my garden when right then and there I could see through the crack in the fence that she was getting a new washer and dryer. I just happened to be right out there and then I see those delivery men lugging them in. She must have got into another big fight with her husband. Oh God, your sister's not gonna know the price of that one."

Nosey Nellie was right. She wouldn't know the price for such a lavish home appliance. We went to the Laundromat. A brunette Bob Barker asked my sister: "Yvonne give us your bid," and she guessed one thousand dollars 'cause Mama always said as she'd carry her load up the steps to Laundryland, "God, I'd give a thousand bucks to have a washing machine right now." And now my sister had bid a thousand dollars.

After all the other contestants made their bids, Bob Barker announced that it was not my sister but someone else who would be getting the shiny brand new deluxe washing machine. But my mama said all was not lost and that my sister had at least two more chances.

Next was a microwave. Fat Fabiola yelled out, "Oh God, she's gonna lose that too. What's with your sister? Didn't she watch the show before she went on? Doesn't she know the prices of things? She should have went on *Wheel of Fortune*. Beto's son went on that and he got lots of nice things for his mother."

My sister again bid one thousand and again she bid too high. Stupid neighbor friend, Patty Romero, stuck her elbow in my stomach and asked "What's with your sister? Is *she* too high? Get it? Get it?"

The last item my sister could bid on was scuba gear. The announcer explained: ". . . to explore the fascinating world of underwater including tanks, regulators, snorkels, backpacks and fins." We couldn't remember the last time we had went scuba diving. We were dead. She *was* gonna come home with nothing.

Charlie Romero, the tall Mexican, said, "Oh that's like what I used when I did Lincoln High's version of *The Man From Pt. Dume*. I wore fins just like that. Man, I should be there on television. Your sister, her body movements are all wrong. She's not bidding with the assertiveness or confidence, any actor knows that. That's why she's losing. She doesn't have the confidence of a winner."

My sister bid one thousand dollars and lost out to the woman next to her who bid nine hundred and ninety dollars.

Fat Fabiola said "Oh, she's coming back with nothing. She never gonna get to The Showcase Showdown. All the way to L.A. and she's coming back with nothing."

But Fat Fabiola was wrong. My sister did get something. One month later a large brown box arrived at our house filled with consolation prizes. They didn't console us one bit. We were the embarrassment of the neighborhood. We got a lifetime supply of Hawaiian Tropic suntan oil and she got a royal blue White Stag jogging suit which she had asked for in her white boyfriend's size (who later really did go *stag* and left her it to sell at a future garage sale).

But the best was a Beta Max video cassette recorder. We were the first one on the block to have one. Nosey Nellie came over to see it and said "Thank God you got that machine. Thank God, now the next time your loser sister is gonna be on TV we can tape it like everyone else in the world."

But we didn't care what anyone said. We felt wonderful knowing that Beta Max would be around for a long time. We felt somewhat like cutting edge pioneers in that mid '70s video technology revolution. We plugged it into our nineteen inch and for months letting the "twelve-zero-zero" flash on the lower right corner, we bragged and bragged to neighbors and friends about the day my sister was on television.

EL CIELO OR BUST

Very soon
Great-aunt Linda
is going to die.

I know this
'cause she's shown me
how to care for her good china,
told me where she keeps
her grandma's wedding ring
and put the pink slip
to Uncle Willie's Buick
in my name.
"Just in case," she says.

She now speaks kindly
of Conchita and Louie,
(past enemies
who did her wrong
many, many years ago)
thinks Warlord,
the pitbull,
had it easy being put to sleep.
And thick, musty drapes
always drawn
make her once sunny home
dark,
sterile,
cold,

like the coffin
she will lie in
soon.

Every other day
before *Dos Mujeres, Un Camino*
after *Wheel of Fortune*,
a uniformed woman
in rosary beads and name badge
comes to Aunt Linda,
comes to bring her IT.
The wafer,
the key,
that will unlock that gate,
her final destination,
last trip,
no senior discount needed to
El Cielo.
That faraway place
high above shake-shingle rooftops,
El Rio water tower.
And just like every 1940s film
on channel 15 promises,
there she will go,
up an angel hair path
leading to some glorious
Hollywood harp shaped gate.

And then I'll miss Aunt Linda,
real bad.
Her untouched guest soaps,
Noxema fresh smell,
crochet dollies every Christmas,
Arthritic fingers,

aching over making
strawberry shortcake supreme.
So gotta keep doing
all the good things
told to me
'cause someday,
at the gate,
Great aunt Linda,
Great uncle Willie,
and Warlord
will be ready and awake
waiting to welcome ME.

A BELATED VICTORY (FOR US)

Reesie B. cornered me good that day.
I cursed,
under my breath,
the teacher who held me in detention
so I had to walk
the home route alone.

"Hhhhey . . .
Wanna see something?
Wanna see something real good?"
he taunted me.

I knew what something was
tried to ignore him
the way my mama does
when men
in back of pickup trucks
hiss at her.

He persisted,
ugly blue bicycle
duct tape on the banana seat,
zigzagging
in front of me,
blocking my path.

"Hhhhey . . .
Can't you hear me?

I'm talking to YOU,
stupid Mexican!"
His words caused welts,
but I couldn't speak.
He was a ninth grader,
a boy,
I was in seventh,
a girl.
No such thing as talking back.

The primered Chevy
with the loose muffler,
I always made fun of
came rumbling toward us.

My Getaway.

I flagged the driver down.
Our neighbor, Mrs. Macías, stopped.
Quickly, I dived
into a safety net of
torn, faded upholstery.

"Mexicans
always have the rattiest cars!"
Reesie B. yelled after us.

"Just ignore him, mi'ja.
He'll never amount to
anything,"
Mrs. Macías predicted.

But I was afraid.
Afraid of this kid

who spent more time in the arcade
than in school,
who laughed after yelling,
"La Migra!"

in the E.S.L. classes.
Was he right?
Will I own a ratty car
when I'm older?
Will I always be afraid of
big, white men,
always looking for a car to flag down?

Twelve years later,
visiting home,
I saw
blocking the doorway
to Bob's Market,
THE BIKE.
I heard that familiar voice,
get louder,
closer.
I tensed up
cleared the way,
as Reesie B. "the man"
swung his big body
onto a bite-size bike.

He peddled away,
yelling over his shoulder
"Stupid Mexicans!

I'll just find someone who thinks
my checks ARE good!"

And suddenly,
I was no longer afraid
of him.

DEAR DIARY

The repulsive repetition of
dry heaves and
regurgitation
woke me up.
I got up from bed
and saw out the window
my newest lover
balancing on bent knees
vomiting in the landlord's garden.
Housemate, Angela, entered
my room
still in a robe with
two mugs of coffee and
together we witnessed
the murder,
my favorite rose bush
with his internal anguish.
She smiled and said
"Found your diary, didn't he?
And just like the others
took advantage of your sound sleep
and read the thing,
didn't he?"
No response was needed
as his acidic insides
of spaghetti, corner liquor store wine
last night's *last* dinner
splattered every

stem, petal and thorn.
We sipped our coffee
watched my new ex-lover
wipe mouth
swagger to parked convertible
and slowly drive away.
"Don't worry,"
Angela said,
"there'll be others."

I saw the yellow belly lining clusters
he left behind,
"Yeah," I agreed,
"but it was this rose bush
I liked best."

THE SUPERHERO SCAM

Batman has a small penis.
I know this
'cause Marsha,
head cashier,
told me.
She had a stint
as an El Torito waitress
years ago.
And in he walked
Pre bat, Mr. Mom,
No entourage
or anything.
Just Mr. B. himself
for chicken fajitas
or something.
Anyway,
he liked either the blond hair
or how brown polyester
hugged her ass,
next thing she knew
she was up in the hills,
Hollywood Hills that is.
Dry humping,
zipper friction
causing sparks.
But
he never let her see
the Bat Dick

in bright light
and now we all know why.
cause batman has a small
penis.
How I pity
those who try to outsmart
sensory perception.
How I pity poor Marsha
misled by Hollywood hype.

Couldn't bear to see Batman II,
knowing what she knew.
Then trade papers tattled:
"Popeye Has Herpes,
Girlfriend Sues!"
Superman dead again.
Where have all the superheroes gone?
Any real men left?

Poor Marsha,
maybe Wonderwoman
will come thru her checkout line.

STUFF

I was all set to write Angela off for good today. That's one of the things I really try to do best in my life, write people off. From one little screw-up to the major straw that breaks this camel's back, I try to keep my friends as temporary as my patience. I guess "friend" isn't really the proper word here—perhaps "People that annoy me the least," or "People that keep me from watching too much TV," better yet "People I really don't want to write off because someday in the future I may need something from them." I put up with all kinds of crap people dish out just 'cause I worry what I may lose out on if I lose them. There's a real thought process involved when it comes to me deciding who'll remain in my life and who'll become history, but with Angela, the choice has been made. I've had it with her. She's always late. I mean *always*. Here it was already a quarter after three, and she still wasn't at my house. She just got back from Louisiana yesterday and made such a big deal about wanting to see me and everything. What a liar. I've known her all my life and never, once, has she been on time. I'm so sick of it, but I knew today was the last day I'd ever have to put up with her. As I waited for her car to drive up my street, I thought of all the people I put up with. The list seemed endless.

Take my friend NeNe. She pisses me off all the time, real bad. Doesn't even matter to say exactly what she does, but it involves my boyfriend Gene's hair and the fact that she's a hairstylist. Hairstylists are the worst, always reaching out and touching your hair, not even asking first. With a wrinkled nose, they're always asking who cut it last, asking if you use salon only products and telling you how they and only they alone can improve its current condition. Anyway, NeNe touches Gene's hair way too many times and I've just about had it. Anytime I say something about it in a joking way, she says "What? Don't be so possessive! I'm a hair artist; this is my craft, I'm working my craft!" and she goes on stroking his hair, talks about rubbing mango chutney through it to stimulate his scalp. Man, now that really burns me up, but I know if I ever decide to get serious with her and pull her aside to tell her, "Look, I'm the only woman in my boyfriend's life who'll ever stimulate him, so why don't you make like scissors and get the hell out of our life!" she'd get all upset and never speak to me again. Then I'd lose all contact with her and her older brother Mike. As his name implies, he is a mechanic. Works out of an independent Swedish dealership in Santa Monica. Probably the only Mexican I know who works on Volvos on the Westside and wears clogs to work. I drive a Honda, but still, he knows how to do everything to a car, I mean *everything*, and he promised when my car reaches 100,000 miles, he'll give it a good work over, real good. I remember his promise every time NeNe reaches for Gene's hair. If I don't keep my mouth shut, I'll end up dishing out big bucks to some unknown grease monkey in the Yellow Pages.

Oh man, which reminds me of another annoying person I know, J. Walker. He's one of those self promoting untalented rocker/musician types who names himself after every alcoholic weakness he happens to have at the time. Two months ago he was J. Daniel, and during May he called himself J. Cuervo, thinking his stupid band would get more Cinco de Mayo gigs or something. What an idiot! All he does is talk about himself and his new band of the week. "The next big thing," he tells me, "we're talking first out

of the gate and into the lead turbo rock-and-roll action!"
Like I really care! He never asks about me, how I'm doing,
what's going on with school, my life . . . nothing. He's always swinging by my work just to see if I'll give him free
fries or something. The whole time he's talking he's playing
with the little silver-plated iron cross trinket that hangs from
a chain his ex-girlfriend bought for him. The ex-girlfriend
he just had to let go 'cause, "Hey, she was getting just too
serious, and I'm a horny guy, a musician, a stallion who can't
be lassoed!" Give me a break! Something about grown men
who identify themselves with hoofed animals and play with
their jewelry while they talk really scares me, but I put up
with it and will continue to put up with it cause this person,
this "friend," has a day job over at a Xerox place in the
valley. Honestly, come on, who can turn down color Xerox
two-sided prints for FREE? I mean anything I want. Full
access no-questions-asked rein to unlimited flyers, spiral
binding, laser printouts, special typeset . . . I name it, I get
it. I have to remind myself this every time I have to listen
to him talk about himself, playing with his charm necklace.

Anyway, back to Angela. It was already four PM and our
date was for two. Man, I couldn't wait to terminate our
friendship this afternoon. Her treatment shows no respect, ab-
solutely no respect to me. But there's so much involved. Besides being a childhood playmate, blood sister, and, really, the
only one who bothered to show me how to use a tampon
correctly, there's only one good reason why I wouldn't write
her off and that's because Angela's mom owns a recreational
vehicle, which means she travels—A LOT. She loves to show
off her worldliness by plastering the back of their RV with
stickers from every state she's visited. Everything from a great
big Georgia Peach decal to a hooting Texan cowboy rub-on.
She's been everywhere! She has almost forty-one emblems to
brag about, and from every one of those, the forty-one states

she's been to, she's brought me back a snow dome. I love snow domes! You know, those round plastic globes, miniature state historical landmark replica placed inside, and when you shake it, hundreds of mini snowchips float around it. I'm nine domes away from having a complete United Domes of America set. Only nine away and if I blow her off today, I'll never have a true set, and to me that's one of the most important things in my life right now.

Which makes me think, you know, I know why people have other people in their lives. Not for love, companionship, nurturing or any of that human need crap that they feed you in psychology class. The real reason we have people in our lives is because we want stuff, free stuff, and we'll put up with all kinds of shit to get it; we will lie to get what we want. From my Chilean girlfriend, Marta, who tells the pay parking lot attendant she's Peruvian just like him so she can park for free to my Aunt Dolly who makes Cousin Amy slouch to an under-twelve-years-of-age size so she can get a price break on a Happy Steak meal. Everybody likes a deal, and then to brag about it later to some *sucker* who paid full price or spent the normal required waiting period to get it—that's the best! We all have it. We all have the same kiss-ass mentality. What a really lousy way to live!

This self-realization overwhelmed me but at least I'd made myself aware of this, and I could do something about it, change my own pattern. No more would I put up with people's crap. I would say exactly how I feel, get them out of my life before it's too late.

Just then I saw Angela turn the corner onto my street. I didn't care how long I'd known her, that at age thirteen we pricked our fingers, that someday she'll be my maid of honor or that she and only she alone could complete my snow dome collection. She's really a lousy friend. I missed my prom 'cause my date and I double-dated with her and her creep of a boyfriend. And again, she was late. I've missed concerts, buses, the first fifteen minutes of every film I've seen with her, missed the eulogy to my own mother's funeral because of her. I hate her. I truly do. Her friendship to me is no longer valid, not worth it.

She pulled up into my driveway, beeping her car horn. I smiled to myself, thinking, "This will be the last time your lazy late-ass car honks in my driveway." She walked toward me, all apologetic like and everything.

"Sorry I'm late. Please don't be mad," she said. "Hey, look, look what I've bought you." She was holding a white paper bag, and inside I looked. The most beautiful sight ever seen, a big green alligator with a clear plastic belly, inside two baby alligators playing on a teeter totter that said "New Orleans," bright orange letters, snowflakes floating all around. I really wanted this snow dome bad. I mean my hands started sweating with anticipation. I wanted to take it from her, but I knew I'd never respect myself if I did. She certainly wasn't gonna let me keep it after I told her what a crummy friend she'd been all my life. I felt confused, I wanted to make a final statement, but I really wanted this snow dome, and as I started to open my mouth, she spoke. "Guess what, Mitchie? I'm going to Europe with my mom next summer! Can you believe it? My graduation gift instead of a new car! Can you imagine what kind of snow domes they have there? You'll have a collection from around the world!"

I smiled the fake smile I'm so good at as she put her arms around me to give me a hug. "I'm really gonna miss you though, three whole months away from my best friend."

I stood there letting her hug me. I felt so lousy, but a lot less confused. I started to hug her back thinking about "patience being a virtue," "taking the good with the bad," "you gotta have friendship!" Finally I took the bag from her hands and felt Angela's chest sigh with relief. It was just that easy.

MR. AND MRS. WHITE GUILT

Own a home north of Wilshire
and open their back door
to every minority issue
they can get their
jeweled freckled hands on.

Patrons of the Arts.

The longer one has been:
incarcerated,
deprived,
abused,
suffering,
the better!

African,
Latino,
Third world kitsch,
Mr. and Mrs. W. G.
will host a fund raiser in honor
of their select pet minority
who is
bad-ass,
raving mad,
confused,
threatening,

and that's the way they like them.

As long as it stays in artistic format,
and as long as they enter
through the back door.

MR. BOOM BOOM MAN

Here he comes!
Distorted bass
nearly three blocks away
announces the coming attraction.
I wait,
at the mercy of the traffic light
waiting
and waiting
for it to change
from red to green
so I won't have to deal with
HIM . . .
Mr. BOOM BOOM Man.

But my rearview mirror
doesn't lie
and pumping his system
from my behind
I see his calling card
baby lavender twinkle lights
hugging a chrome-plated license plate
five-digit proclamation:
OO-BAD
coming at *me*!

His fifty-pound medallion
heaving hickey-stained neck
closer to the center of his manhood:

his beeper.
He pulls up slowly,
lowered Nissan mini truck
fills the vacancy on my left,
and as the automatic tinted window
makes its slow way down,
I start to wonder
"Why can't I be like the cool girls
and like the cars that go:
BOOM BA BOOM . . . ?

Dig the way quarters
bounce off vinyl roofs?"
"Funky, fresh, and stoooopid,"
they say.

But then a flash of gold
blinds my thoughts
and Mr. BOOM BOOM,
shouts out:
"Hey,
sen-yo-reeeeta!
mamacita!
you speak English?
hey . . . YOU!
I'm talkin' to you,
deaf bitch!"
        Then I remember.
I wanna yell out,
"Yeah, I speak English,
Pig Latin too
so uckfay offay Mr. BOOM BOOM!
Take your fade
and f-f-fade away!"

But I don't have the time
(or the balls).

The light has turned green.
I take off,
FAST!
leaving behind
Mr. BOOM BOOM
Bu-foon.

THE REAL ME

The kids next door are on acid
again.
They are tripping,
marveling how they can see
right through
my landlord's garbage can,
its filthy contents
in full color spectrum
and how each vein
in each leaf
of our neighbor's maple tree
is intensified.

I put off checking the mailbox
for fear that their
almighty psychedelic power
will enable them to see
right through ME,
the real me:
gray chalky skin stuffed
into J. C. Penney panties
with broken elastic.

THE BEST YEARS OF MY LIFE

Somewhere
my vomit lays
in petrified clusters
off Rose Ave. in El Rio.
Every weekday morning
my mother
grandfather
neighborhood carpool parent
pulled over
swung the passenger door
open
wide
QUICKLY
so I could flush out
the post jr. high anxiety
that in my belly
fiercely tap danced
with sugar Pop Tarts and
blood red chorizo.

Once my mouth
was sleeve clean
the journey continued
the last mile
the long mile
to that secondary holding facility:
Rio Mesa High School.
Where every day

my stomach and I
battled
acid damaged 'nam vets
who taught calculus
Bio lab instructors flirting
with wealthy white girls
whose fathers owned country clubs
they so badly wanted to join.
School officials with unofficial titles
Dean of all Dicks and Birdlegs Barnet
power played with students
tagged "Weedboy Willie" and "La Spooky."
Monica Winters wanting
badly
to kick my ass
'cause I wouldn't give in
to the pharmaceuticals
she carried
in her stolen Gucci bag.

This place
had
Hawaiian day
Pajama day
'60s day.
Everyone played the part
dressed the part
but everyday
I wore the costume
the fears of this clown
that someday over the loud speaker
Dean of all Dicks
would announce:
"Tomorrow will be inner-self day.

Come as your true self."
Then I'd be caught.
I'd be dead.
How would I explain
to Tia Annie's confused hands
to sew me a costume
portraying me
the real me
latch-key emptiness
suicidal contemplation
internal jellyfish canker sores
stinging and sucking
the last of my school girl esteem
nothing no
over the counter chocolate chalk
or weekend in Ojai could ever
soothe coat and protect?

Every day
I dragged my feet
in customized black and pink Vans
(only thing about me
the right color, right size)
slipping through Mary the hall monitor
Petey, student super narc
to the girl's bathroom
to find an empty stall
a toilet to sit on
to wait
and wait
for the three o'clock bell to ring.

PLANNED PARENTHOOD: AGE SIXTEEN

The devil's workshop
located indiscreetly
between aging five-and-dime
and neo-European outdoor cafe.
Young girls
enter, exit and enter again
through taped-up glass doors
on the hour, every half hour
holding precious brown bag
filled with pills
that promise reliable worry-free bliss.
Inside
I am surrounded by posters
that plead for safe-sex awareness,
angry phone rings
screaming for attention,
young legs enveloped in
stone-washed denim
shaking nervously.

As a child,
my catechism teacher warned me,
"If you walk too close
or look too long
in the direction of the sin clinic,
your soul will be contaminated!"
In jr. high,
worldly Anna Chavez taught me,

"Only putas go on the pill."
Discerning Aunt Marla preached,
"Sexual activity begins after marriage.
Any questions, ask your husband."
Maybe the reasons why,
again,
I'm the minority
in a sea of blond and green eyes.
Equal only 'cause,
separately, we share
student status,
parental fear,
having a lover (or two).

Shunning the wise words
from my past,
I take the questionnaire
cross out "other"
to pencil in "woman of color,"
and wait for my name to be called.

THE GRUDGE-HOLDERS

My Great-grandpa Louie has died. It doesn't even matter to say if he was my mother's grandfather or my dad's. He belonged to everyone. Everyone loved Grandpa Louie. Everyone spoke to him, and when I say that, I mean that no one held grudges against him.

I took my roommate, Angela, to his funeral. She offered to drive the long distance. "This is gonna be difficult," I told her in the car.

"Death is difficult," she replied.

"No, it isn't that . . . It's my family. I come from a long line of grudge-holders. Nobody speaks to each other. When a certain somebody enters the room, a certain somebody leaves the room. If I had a turnstile that popped out a nickel every time someone went through it in a huff, I would be a millionaire."

"Oh God, it can't be that bad. This is death, human tragedy. Stuff like this brings people together, especially family."

"You don't know *my* family," I said, seeing a fast food drive-thru in the distance. "Hey, pull up through there. I'm hungry."

When we finally got to my grandma's house, Angela looked around. "Hey, it doesn't seem so bad. Everyone seems together."

"Oh no, Angela, it's only certain ones, but their stubborn blood taint the rest, makes everyone sick. The little ones catch on early, and the tradition is handed down generation to generation . . ."

Angela laughed, "Mexicans are so funny. It's always a pride thing with you guys."

"Not pride," I corrected. "Principle, it's the principle of the matter," pointing out my cousin, Linda. "See her? About two years ago her parents, my Uncle Charlie and Aunt Rosie, promised her a new car for her sixteenth birthday. Three days before her birthday, Uncle Charlie had to break the news to her. They just couldn't afford the car. He tells her this three days before her birthday. Months after she had been bragging to all her friends about her new Mustang 5.0. She promised to take her friends dancing in L.A. and everything! She looked like a fool in front of everyone. She swore she would never talk to her father again. And, as far as I know, she hasn't."

Angela said, "But she's just a kid. Teenagers do that sort of stuff all the time. She'll get over her high school grudge."

"Don't you bet on it," I told her.

I pointed out my other cousin, Lupita. "You see her? That's my cousin Lupita. She's been on a diet as long as I've known her. She's tried everything to lose those thirty extra pounds. But they'll always be there. It's just her. She's wasted so much money on diet programs, therapy, surgery . . . you name it. She just gains it all back. One time she was down to one-forty and looking pretty good. But then my uncle Chuy saw her and started singing, 'Lupita, Lupita, still a gordita . . .' Man, was she pissed. I told her to ignore him, that's just the way he is. But she said, 'No, I'm not gonna forget that. He's a grown man. He should know better. Everyone always says, "That's just the way he is". . . . and they let him get away with murder. Somebody should tell him he's wrong. But it won't be me because I will never speak to him again,' and she hasn't."

"Well, I can understand that," said Angela. "I mean, I'm real sensitive about my weight . . . but still, she should have told him. It seems the grudge-holders in your family are the women."

"No," I corrected her again, "the men are just as bad, if not worse." I point out Uncle Eddie who's on one side of the room and my uncle Lalo who's on the other. "See, my uncle Eddie doesn't speak to Lalo. It all started many years ago when they were just little kids. Their father, my great uncle Eddie, took them to the park. They came across one of those pony rides. You know, one ride for a quarter? My great uncle was poor back then. He didn't have enough money for both so he said they would have to flip for it. So he flipped a coin, probably the only coin he had, and said, 'Little Eddie, heads, Lalo, tails.' When the coin landed on the ground it showed heads, which meant Eddie should have gotten the ride, but Lalo grabbed that coin quick and yelled, 'Tails! I win!' and ran off to ride the pony. Just like that. My uncle Eddie says that whole experience was real traumatic for him. And it just proved how selfish his younger brother was and still is. My uncle Lalo, when he started making money even bought Eddie's kids a horse, but Uncle Eddie doesn't care. He says his 'inner child' is still wounded and that he'll never have anything to do with Lalo again."

By this time Angela looked exhausted. She didn't want to hear anymore. She just wanted to eat. I pulled out a bag from my backpack.

"What's that?"

"It's food, from the burger place," I told her.

"I'm sure there's gonna be food here, isn't there?"

"Oh, yeah, there will be," I assured her, "lots of it . . . pozole, enchiladas, sopes . . . good stuff like that. But we can't eat any of it."

"Why not?"

"Because my aunt Alma made it. She once talked trash about my mother right before she died. I mean, right there my mother is dying and she says, 'I knew this was coming. Your mother never took care of herself properly and who's really suffering? Her? No. Me? No. *It's you,* that's who . . . all alone in the world. Your mother did this to you.' There she was telling me something like that. I swore, right there and then, I would never speak to Aunt Alma again."

"I don't want to hear anymore," Angela said. "Let's just eat."

I handed her a bag of fries and a burger. She unwrapped it, lifted up the hamburger bun and then curled her lip in disapproval. "What?" I asked.

"It's a double cheese supreme. You know I don't like cheese. You've known me what, nine, ten years and you still can't remember that I hate cheese? This is so like you. Just like on my eighteenth birthday, you showed up with that birthday cake lathered in butter cream frosting. Butter cream is for kids, just for babies. You know I had wanted sour-cream frosting. I had been hinting a whole week earlier. My first birthday as legal adult and you show up with baby butter cream."

I couldn't believe this! "Your *eighteenth* birthday? Angela, that was five years ago! You're still holding on to that? Butter cream frosting? You *are* a baby!"

She threw the hamburger into my lap and ran to my grandma's bathroom, squeezing the space between her eyes. "Go ahead, run away!" I yelled after her, "I have nothing to be sorry about, NOTHING. Baby . . . big baby wannabe grudge-holder and you aren't even Mexican!"

I looked around. Nobody in my family paid attention to my yells or her dramatic exit and this bummed me out. What's the point of making a point and nobody pays attention?

Reluctantly I laid out my fast food picnic on my grandma's shag carpet and began to chomp on cold French fries and two greasy burgers in that room full of principle. Meanwhile my young cousin, Linda, ate in the kitchen, separately from her parents, cousin, Lupita, took her second helpings outside and ate alone. The bookends, Lalo and Eddie, stood their ground all macho like at opposite ends of my grandma's living room.

And my Great grandpa Louie, sat in heaven, looking down, laughing at us all.

MANOS MORENAS

Maria is a poet
but it is her hands
that speak the memories

The Chilean activist/artist
held mine
as he tongue fed me
homemade wafer cookies
in between overdone kisses.
"You have working hands,"
he whispered.
I pulled away
embarrassed
of my calloused income.
He took them back
assuring me,
"You don't want
to look like those
gabachas on Wilshire
manicured and ready
. . . to do nothing."

My co-worker, Yolie,
shook her head in shame
at the sight of these fingers:
"No color
no tips

no wedding band.
A woman
is as good as her
porcelain set
and the rock
a man gives her
to wear."

Between a flagging career
and city college night courses,
my mother's
own tired hands
patted homemade masa
coaxed roses out of dead soil
nurtured two babies
typed term papers till
three in the morning
never clenched a bottle neck
or leather belt
free of nicotine stains
seldom lifted a paintbrush
but died an artist.

I remember
all of this
when I see Maria's hands.

THE GIFT

ust as promised, the brown delivery truck pulled up a little after three P.M. that Friday afternoon. My mother called out: "It's here! Come look!"

I got up from the television to help my mother meet three sweaty men in khaki uniforms. We played like ladies, watching helpless and from a distance as the moving men heaved the large solid object closer and closer to our front door. "God, it's really a monster," I said to myself.

My mother heard me. "It's not a monster. It's a desk. But not just any old desk, this is a *writer's* desk." She pointed out that under the thick mahogany roll top there were secret compartments, so many spacious drawers, slots for letters, organizers . . . this desk had everything. She handed me a key that would lock my privacy away from the outside world and my sister. "Only you will have this key," she told me as she wrapped my fingers around it. "Make a copy and hide it somewhere no one will find it."

I looked down at that special key, and then watched my mother fuss about, directing the men to the vacuumed empty corner of my small room. My mother was really serious about this writing thing and it concerned me. You see, from when I was a little kid, say seven or eight years old, I always bragged about what a great writer I was going to be. My plan was to write the great American novel, the literary achievement that would get me ten years on the best-sellers list—the kind of book that would be confiscated out of high school hands by frustrated English teachers, a book that would make big macho men sob, keep newlywed husbands restless as they anxiously waited for young newlywed wives to finish its last chapter by bedside light. Yes, everyone would want my book. But there I was, almost twelve years old and there my mother was, getting a little too serious about *my* dream. I felt panic as I saw the last mover hand over a payment contract to my mother. I heard her tell my father about the extra hours she was going to work to help pay for this desk. I knew exactly what that meant. It meant no more family Friday night KFC dinners anymore. No more Saturday mall excursions, big Sunday breakfasts and no more night school art classes for her. She would not be around. She would not have time. She would have to be at work weekends, working and working to pay for that extra bill, the bill for the desk, my desk. But none of this mattered to her.

"You are a writer," she reminded me. "A desk like this is essential and you need the best tools to work with. You have a gift." She wrapped her thick arms around me, and as I inhaled her mama smell of Jungle Gardenia and yardwork sweat, I thought about how much I really loved my mother. She had so much faith in me. She then walked over to the desk, wiped away unseen dust with her sleeve and then made her way to the garage to get a metal folding chair. She could not afford the matching mahogany one.

That weekend, everyone came to see my desk. My uncle Charlie shook his head and let out a long slow whistle when he first saw it: "Man, you *better* write something good on that thing!" he threatened. "With all that money your mother is spending, she could've gotten you and your sister a couple of mopeds. Maybe three of them! Mopeds are really big now. Not really a bike or a motorcycle, but a *mo*-ped. Get it? I got my kids one and they love it. They aren't into books and writing poetry and all that kind of stuff. Nah, they just like to ride around on their mopeds. Not really going anywhere, just around, you know."

My sister's comments were more clear and to the point. First she glared at the desk, then at me, then back to the desk and said, "It's because of THAT, we aren't getting the swimming pool."

My lousy neighbor friend, Patty Romero, crinkled her eyebrows at the sight of my new desk: "Why did you get a desk so big?" she asked. "And it's so dark! My dad got me a real nice study desk and it's lightweight too. Fits right under my bed at night. He painted it up real pretty, light pink paint left over from the bathroom he did last week. It looks real nice . . . you know, your desk looks like an old man's desk, yeah, that's it, sort of like the one at my doctor's. Oooh, I hate going to the doctor. I wouldn't want my room looking like his office."

I really hated Patty. She was always saying stupid things. Like when I told her of my plans of becoming a big famous writer and that someday my stories would make me rich and I would buy a new car for my mother. She rolled her eyes and laughed at me. "Oh brother! That is so stupid. That is so stupid to think that way. You think you're gonna be someone so great, like that guy, the singer, what's his name? That *La Bamba* guy who bought his mom a house with his record money. You are nothing like him! Nothing. Except that maybe you both can't speak Spanish . . . Your poor mom, she's gonna be waiting forever for her car."

Oh my God. Patty was right. I didn't have the talent, the imagination, the knowledge, the inspiration to write. Who was I kidding? My mother wasted her money. I looked at the desk and thought of all the great things our family could have had . . . a moped (or two), a swimming pool, a pink fold-away desk. I was so mad at what everyone was saying. Who did they think they were, telling me things like that?

I would prove them wrong, all wrong, starting first thing Monday, the great novel would begin . . .

And so it began, the start of that week, my first attempts at the great novel. During that month of May, I would come home, skipping the New Mickey Mouse Club, fun time with bestfriend Goony, to sit at the desk waiting, waiting to be inspired. What would I write about? I'd never traveled, never been in love, never experienced some great tragedy, the three main elements a writer must experience in order to be successful. I didn't know any of them. Oh man, who was I kidding? I didn't have the stuff to be a writer. Then I thought maybe I could write like someone else, not really copy, but sorta have the same style, but in my own way. Let's see, who could I write like? My mother liked John Steinbeck. He was her idol. He seemed easy enough. I cried at the end of *The Grapes of Wrath*, and what about *Tortilla Flats*? The name alone told me this Steinbeck guy was very much like me. I like to cry and I like tortillas. Oh, this writing thing was in my blood. All I needed was time and with summer less than a few weeks away, I would have plenty of time. I was going to make her so proud. I would make the whole family proud. I pushed myself away from the desk and gave myself a brand new deadline. By September I would be the next great American writer. I had plenty of time.

But as that summer passed, I did everything but write the great American novel. Sure, I sat at the desk and wrote, but nothing that would ever make a best-sellers list . . . I wrote eight-page letters to newly discovered *Tigerbeat Magazine* idols, postcards to pen pals in Africa and Malaysia, sonnets for lonely arthritic aunts up north and unmailed letters to my father, who had left, asking him to please move back home.

It was a pattern, a kind of game, really. Every summer,

every season of every year, I would spend so much time at that desk, pretending to be the great writer. When I entered jr. high, I used the desk to write book reports, other people's book reports, ten dollars for ten pages (I never felt an ounce of guilt and never knew I was getting ripped off). The game continued, summer, fall, spring . . . pretending, pretending . . . there was always an excuse. My junior year, an English teacher told the class that writers write every day. Again, another reminder that I wasn't doing my job, and so I really tried my best to fit the bill. I mean, I called myself a writer, didn't I? I started to stay up late on week nights, sitting and sitting at the desk, paper and pen in hand. Sometimes my mother would look in from my bedroom door and smile. She looked so pleased. Little did she know I was really practicing her signature from a canceled check so I could forge another absentee note for school. The desk became such a fixture in my life: on it I made bio. lab cheat sheets, filled out college applications, stuffed money orders into parking-ticket envelopes, did my EZ tax form, and practiced a glamorous signature for those future book-signing parties . . . I did everything at that desk, but write IT, the book, The Novel, the down payment to my mother's new car.

Finally, after high school, sick of so many weak attempts at junior college and part-time jobs, I moved out of my mother's home. I needed to live somewhere, well, where writers live, which meant the big city, any big city. I took the important things with me, but of course not the desk. My mother asked: "What about your desk? How are you going to write? Aren't you going to take it?"

I didn't want to take the thing. It was such a nuisance, a reminder that I was a failure, a reminder of my aborted attempts at fiction. Why had my mother bought me such a desk? Who did she think she was, buying a kid such a lavish gift, only to have it haunt that kid for the rest of her life?

My mother could have her stupid desk, I'll never make room for it in my life, *Never!* And I didn't. So, there it sat, year after year, gathering dust, parked in that vacuumed back corner, that back corner of my room. My mother never said anything else about it, and I never said anything else about it. From then on every visit home, the reality set in: I was not a writer. I never wrote anything.

Then it happened, a human tragedy . . . death. The third element to make a writer more experienced with life and pain. But this was *my* mother's death, smack! Ten-day warning on Mother's Day and then she was gone. I mean, just like that. My mother, my mom, my mama. And the ceremony began, somber lines of distant relatives who embraced and consoled, huge pots of *pozole* heated on grandma's gas stove, sympathy cards with promises of "we are here for you" but they weren't and they aren't, 'cause people have lives and people are busy, busy giving reasons and excuses for not doing things they should be doing, giving excuses like me.

After the ceremony, I went back to my old bedroom in that now hollowed out home on Orange Drive in Oxnard. I sat at the desk that had grown so incredibly small over the years. I ignored the thick depths of dust that had gathered and waited. The last of the ceremony was still to come.

The sound of car brakes outside interrupted my thoughts, and I looked out the window. The moving men were back. They parked their truck in the driveway and started to unload boxes from the back of the truck. In their khaki uniforms, they came in carrying my mother's Styrofoam-packed life in cardboard boxes, fifty-two years in over fifty-two crates. I stepped out of my room so they could enter. I watched from a distance as they wiped the sweat from their foreheads. There were so many to carry and not much room to store them. One of the movers said, "If they got rid of that desk, we'd have more room." I said nothing as I watched them improvise with the desk's existence. They piled more and more things around it, behind it, on top of it, until the last box was placed by the last mover. He wiped his forehead with his sleeve and handed me a bill.

Finally they were gone, and I was alone. I sat in my room turned depository, amid twenty-year-old Tupperware, half empty bottles of Avon perfume, unfinished sewing projects, photo albums stacked high, tight and around that desk, crushing it to nothing. I made my way to it, pushing away boxes and crates to make a space to sit at it. On a foam-filled carton, I sat thinking of my mother, her gift to me, to work my gift. Why did she have so much faith in my dream of becoming a writer? I thought of the art classes she never went to, my uncle Charlie's kids who no longer have mopeds but who still just drive around and around, not really going anywhere, and I thought of my future kids. Would they be big talkers and no walkers like me, their mother?

There were no more excuses. I cleared away yellowed papers, musty shoe boxes and wiped away dust with my sleeve. In one of the compartments, I found a notepad and some pens and pulled them out. I made a space for some paper and began to write.

ABOUT THE AUTHOR

Michele Serros was born and raised sixty miles north of Los Angeles in Oxnard, California. As a young girl, she was greatly inspired by the writers Louise Fitzhugh, S. E. Hinton, and Judy Blume. She is a big fan of wet burritos, German Expressionist art, and *The X-Files*.